Phyl Frost

Highgate of Beverley

Highgate Press (Markham) Limited
1995

British Library Cataloguing in Publication Data.
A catalogue record for this book is available from the British Library.

ISBN 1 899498 03 6

Published by

Highgate of Beverley
Highgate Press (Markham) Limited
24 Wylies Road, Beverley, HU17 7AP
Telephone (01482) 866826

Produced by

4 Newbegin, Lairgate, Beverley, HU17 8EG
Telephone (01482) 886017

Front Cover Picture: The Molescroft Inn and adjacent houses. (Stephen Robinson)
Back Cover Picture: Molescroft – from Malton Road. (Stephen Robinson)

CONTENTS

Page

PREFACE

This represents my attempt: firstly, to express the significance of Molescroft based on its historic foundations; secondly, to show its development through the ages up to the present day.

Research has been confined to locally available data, general reading and the numerous books and papers detailed in the Bibliography.

I am indebted to Trevor Komaromy of North Milford Hall, Tadcaster, for his supply of information relating to the Leedes family; to Ken Bateman for information relating to Swiss Cottage; to Katie Scott who gave time to tell me about the Molescroft of her younger days; and to others who, by their interest, have provided encouragement.

It is my intention to donate my royalties to St. Leonard's Church, Molescroft.

Phyl Frost

ACKNOWLEDGEMENTS

The special thanks of the author and publisher go to Molescroft Parish Council who made a generous grant towards the costs of this book. Gratitude is also expressed to Mr. M. P. Campey of Mark's Bakery who also gave a much appreciated donation.

Thanks are offered to Mervyn King who kindly provided the sketches – 'Molescroft as imagined' and 'Molescroft Land prior to Enclosure, 1803'.

Also to all who have assisted by the loan of photographs:
Mrs. K. Atkinson,
Pat Deans,
Humberside Leisure Services,
Mansfield Brewery Plc,
Mr. R. V. Tennant,
Jack and Elizabeth Walker.

INTRODUCTION

Molescroft is an area immediately adjacent to the town of Beverley, on its northern side. It is a Civil Parish with a Parish Council although not a separate Ecclesiastical Parish but part of the Parish of St. John, Beverley Minster, and, like other similar areas of Beverley, *i.e.* Tickton and Woodmansey, has a church which is a chapel of ease to the Minster.

In sharp contrast to its early beginnings one sees mainly a modern residential area, but its rural connections are maintained by the retention of some farming. Its public house and a few of its houses provide a link with the past.

In addition, there are two schools – a County Primary and a Comprehensive – plus a College of Further Education. There are, also, seven shops, one of the original six having recently been divided into two.

Longcroft Hall, originally occupied by Mr. J. A. Hudson, now part of Beverley College.

Aerial view of Molescroft, 1989.
Key: 1 Roundabout, 2 Church Road, 3 Church, 4 Molescroft Inn, 5 Longcroft School, 6 Beverley College, 7 Woodhall Way, 8 Playing Field, 9 Shopping Parade, 10 County Primary School. *(Humberside County Council)*

CHAPTER 1

ORIGINS

Molescroft, as we see it today, is unlikely to fill the onlooker with any deep sense of historical background. Surprisingly, however, it goes back more than a thousand years. The first recorded evidence of a settlement in the area is the entry in the Domesday Book of 1086 – which indicates that it must have existed before that date, but it is here that I have to reply on conjecture about its origins.

The name, Molescroft, is said to be of Anglian origin and started out as 'Moll's croft' (meaning enclosure). One can imagine its being a clearing in vast woodland set on high ground away from the wet land to the south and east. The Angles who gave the settlement its name came from Schleswig in Northern Germany and settled in Eastern Britain in the 5th century. Sir Frank Stenton, in his book *Anglo Saxon England*, states:

'In the centre and East of Yorkshire a number of Anglian people had been settled for more than a century before the year 600. The distribution of their recorded burial place suggests that in the heathen time they were settled most thickly in the neighbourhood of the Yorkshire Wolds beneath which, in the plain around Beverley, the name Dera Wudu preserved the memory of their common woodlands.'

A further justification for placing Molescroft's origin in the 5th century is the fact that many Anglo-Saxon burial sites or sepulchre mounds were found in the surrounding area. Some were located at nearby Bishop Burton, and I understand that urns used to hold the ashes of cremated bodies and some implements were recovered from there and are now housed in the British Museum.

An alternative explanation of the derivation of Molescroft is that it was named by the Danes as 'Mulscroft', a Scandinavian name for 'the place on the hill'. If the settlement was founded by the Danes then it would date from the 9th century. Some uncertainty surrounds this theory, however, as there is doubt about the Danes having reached this part of England.

Another factor which draws me to the likelihood of the earlier foundation of the hamlet lies in the probable reason for its continued existence. This relates to a building which has prime importance for the origin of Beverley – the monastery to which John retired in 718. The site of the monastery was discovered by the archaeologists to have been in Lurk Lane close to where the Minster stands today, but the surrounding area would present a very different picture. Marshy ground extended for some distance in the flat low-lying region, making it essential for the monks to find an area suitable for cultivation in order to provide food. The higher ground to the north-west, now known as Molescroft, would provide desirable agricultural land together with, presumably, good hunting ground. This is my own theory – I have traced no recorded facts in support of the idea.

Domesday Book does record, albeit some 300 years later, that the Collegiate Church (formerly the monastery) owned half the land in Molescroft. The entry states:

> '3 carucates for geld + 2 ploughs can be there.
> One moiety is the Archbishop's and the other St. John's.
> 2 villeins have 1 plough there.'

A carucate is equivalent to approximately 100 acres and a plough is a smaller area of ground, the dictionary definition being 'as much land as could be ploughed by one team of light oxen in the year'. As 'one moiety' means a half it seems that the Collegiate Church owned 150 acres. It is interesting to note that 1,400 carucates constituted a parish, and Molescroft fell far short of this.

The name of the hamlet is entered in the form currently used, which is only a slight deviation from its Anglian title. During the next five centuries many different forms or the name have been recorded. In 1120 it appears in the *Chronica Monasteri de Melsa* (*The Chronicle of Meaux Abbey*) as 'Mollescroft', in 1195 it is written in the *Chapter Act Book of Beverley Minster* as 'Mulescroft', and through the centuries it had six changes, ending with an entry in the *Yorkshire Feet of Fines* as 'Mowescroft'. Probably this is merely a demonstration of the lack of uniformity in spelling. It is interesting to learn from Oliver's *History and Antiquities of the Town and Minster of Beverley* (1829) that it was sometimes called 'Mylcroft', probably from the mile-cross which marked the sanctuary limit of the area.

This leads to another factor which may have contributed to the early existence of Molescroft, namely, that its location is likely to have been at one of the principal entrances to Beverley. The 300 acres were, most probably, an area which, in present-day Molescroft, surrounds the junction of the Malton, Driffield, Molescroft and Church Roads. Whether or not mere pathways were the origin of these roads is uncertain, but the fact that there was a sanctuary cross at Molescroft, said to have been situated 'near Leckingfield Park', indicates that a principal road to Beverley came from the direction of Leconfield. The sanctuary cross would follow King Athelstan's granting the right of sanctuary to Beverley and the Minster in 937. The crosses were placed on principal roads one mile distant from the Minster.

I can find nothing in history relating to Molescroft in the next 160 years or so following the Domesday Book entry, apart from the mention that the Abbey of Meaux held 100 acres of land during the latter part of the 12th century. During that period the Abbot was much occupied in acquiring a vast acreage of land, chiefly as pasture for the huge flocks of sheep which the Abbey owned. Judging from later details of land ownership I conclude that the

100 acres lay outside that possessed by the Archbishop and the Collegiate Church and was the beginning of the extension of Molescroft. The size of the population is unknown but the few who lived there were, presumably, employed by the Collegiate Church to cultivate the land and, maybe, there were one or two shepherds working for Meaux Abbey. Some of the land would, in fact, be woodland. The people would live in their small huts built of wattle and daub, probably in the area of the present Church Road.

Woodhall: remains revealed when the site was prepared for building developments, late 1960s.

CHAPTER 2

13th and 14th CENTURIES

The 13th century appears to have been a turning point in the development of Molescroft and interesting snippets include a reference to the fact that in 1236 the Archbishop had a grant of free warren in the area, in other words he had freedom to hunt game. The most significant feature of the time is the first mention of land being occupied. In 1250 the Manor of Woodhall was built by Sir William Woodhall for occupation by Roger Woodhall. It is said to have stood in a square piece of ground adjoining Pighill Lane (Woodhall Way). The *Victoria History of Beverley* (1989) records that by 1803 the house and estate occupied much of the area between Molescroft Road and Woodhall Way. The Manor had many owners. Early in the 14th century it belonged to John Ermyt, followed, in 1371, by Robert de Woodhall, Roger de Woodhall, Sir Edmund de Heslerton, Sir John Heslerton and Sir Thomas Thessed, who made suit at the court of the Bedern for 'this mansion and land in Molescroft'. According to George Oliver's *History and Antiquities of the Town and Minster of Beverley,* the source of the quotation, this information has been extracted from the Provost's book. In the same paragraph he states: 'Five years afterwards (1376) Sir Simon de Heslerton, knight, did homage for the Woodhall juxta Beverley and his land in Molescroft.' (Perhaps he had been omitted from the earlier lengthy list of claimants.) Apparently there were houses near the Woodhall, as, in 1387, Sir Thomas de Sheffield conveyed 'some tenements to Sir Ralph de Heslerton to hold of knights service'. The medieval meaning of knight was one, who, in return for military service, was granted land, in this case houses also.

By the early 14th century there were two more large houses in the vicinity of what is now Woodhall Way: Pighill Hall and the Scrubs. Pighill Hall was in existence by 1312 and was said to have been 'a moated site with a house and its appurtenances belonging to John son of Philip Carter'. In 1347 it passed to John Roos. The Scrubs, whose title indicates that it was in the present Scrubwood Lane area, was also a moated site. In 1312 it was held by Roger Scoter who, in addition, had 'another' house – this was Lane Rack Hall, but its location is unknown. Roger Scoter owned 100 acres of land. In 1316 the houses and land were inherited by Roger Ingleberd (named Lord of Molescroft but, perhaps, a local title for a rich man) and thence by Philip Ingleberd, Rector of Keyingham, who was noted for his founding of two scholarships at University College, Oxford, for 'two scholars or masters born near Beverley'.

Moving along Woodhall Way, perhaps to the area immediately before the sharp bend in the road, we reach the presumed site of a house named Estoft, maybe so called because of its position on the eastern side of Molescroft.

More pictures of remains of Woodhall, uncovered in late 1960s.

Oliver states that 'this was also termed a capital mansion. The foundations of some old buildings at the end of Pighill Lane were dug up in 1824, which probably were the site of this building'. I have been unable to trace the date of origin of the house but, in 1377, ownership, together with lands, passed to William Frost from John Rede, plus a small acreage of land previously belonging to William de Anlaby. All this was granted to William Frost by virtue of his military service.

In the *Yorkshire Archaeological Society – Record Series, Feet of Fines,* there is an entry relating to Walter Frost of 'Kyngeston-upon-Hull' obtaining one messuage (dwelling house) plus one acre of land from John Cokerell and Joan, his wife, in 1375. Walter Frost was the steward to the Archbishop of York, which meant that he held a highly responsible position as manager of the Archbishop's estate. The site of the house is not stated but I am inclined to conclude that it was the one named Woodcroft which was situated near the Molescroft boundary at Gallows Lane.

There were some instances where only land was acquired, presumably rented from the Collegiate Church. At this time the land in Molescroft was owned by the Archbishop and St. John's College (the Minster). In 1290 the estate of the latter was divided between the Chapter and the Provost. The Chapter's portion was assigned to the Prebendary of St. Martin and the Vicars Choral. Such ownership of land conveyed certain rights and privileges known as franchises. The Provost's included the assize (statutory pricing arising from the price regulations introduced in 1266 by Henry III) of bread and ale and the responsibility for waifs and strays. The Chapter's franchises included the escheat of felons, that is, the confiscation of the property of those convicted of serious crimes. By 1303 the Archbishop's holding of land amounted to 200 acres, which was wholly let, and the overlordship passed to Bishop Burton Manor.

In 1312 'a small estate' in Molescroft was held by Killingwoldgraves in a place called Maudlin Riding 'near which was an ancient mill belonging to the Hothams'. 'Killingwoldgraves' relates to the hospital for women which was opened in 1166 on a site about one mile from Bishop Burton. The name of the location of the 'small estate' is interesting: 'Maudlin', presumably, is a mis-spelling of Magdalene, the hospital being dedicated to St. Mary Magdalene, and 'Riding' indicates that the ground was situated near a road suitable for riding, probably a track beside a wood. In 1327 William de Cave de Sancton also had some land in Maudlin Riding for which he did homage and fealty in the Provost's Court. In 1355 Adam Coke and Margaret, his wife, took over the lease of 18 acres of land from Walter de Ake and, in 1371, we find that Ingelram de Nafferton did homage and fealty for 12 acres of land.

Despite the increasing use of land and the building which took place, Molescroft remained a hamlet, described by historians as a liberty of Beverley. The dictionary definition of liberty in this context is 'a district controlled by a city though outside its boundary'. Additionally, it did not qualify for ecclesiastical parish status when such were established in the 10th century because it fell short of the required minimum of 1,400 acres. Hence, no Parish Church in Molescroft.

There was, however, a chantry, dedicated to the Virgin Mary, endowed by Roger Ingleberd some time between 1307 and 1323. It is highly likely that the chantry chapel was situated on the site of the present church, judging from a map of 1803 which shows the area at the junction of the Driffield and Malton Roads named as Chapel Close. The endowment, which was to cover the maintenance costs of the chantry and the stipend of a priest, was met from the leasing of land in Molescroft, Beverley and Paull. Philip Ingleberd was involved, also, with the endowment, probably continuing it after Roger's death. The purpose of the chantry was for the saying of masses, by a priest, for the souls of deceased persons named by the benefactor (chiefly relatives) and for the living, *i.e.* the benefactor and others named by him. The founding of a chantry required a licence from the monarch, who had to be named the first of those for whom masses were to be said. In this case it would be Edward II who, incidentally, visited the Minster on three occasions, 1310, 1316 and 1319. I have not discovered any details of the first chantry priest but there is mention of John de Levenying, 'chaplain of the chantry of the blessed Virgin', obtaining a 'tenement in the same place' (Molescroft) in 1376.

Delivery service in Molescroft in the inter-war years.

Amidst all the changes taking place in Molescroft in the 13th and 14th centuries, including an extension of its boundaries, what of the ordinary people, the villeins or serfs as they were called? No factual details are available because, until the introduction of the Poll Tax of 1377, they would not appear in any official records and it was not until some two centuries later that Church Registers of baptisms, marriages and burials were initiated.

It is likely that they still lived in the area of the original Molescroft, that is, in the present Church Road which, by the 14th century, warranted the name of Towngate or Northgate. The housing would consist of small thatched cottages, self-built, of course, with no chimney, and no glass in the windows. I hope they had shutters when one thinks of the cold winds blowing from the Wolds or from the North Sea. The cottage would be divided into two rooms, one to house animals, the other for human habitation.

The people were dependent for survival on their own efforts so that land was required for their growing of barley, oats and vegetables: hence the strip system, in which a field was farmed in common and divided into strips, each holder having one or more strips. Presumably some of the peasants would be engaged in working the land to supply food for the Collegiate Church as successive generations had been doing but I imagine that the people with the large houses and with land would employ others. The likely jobs would be those of ploughman, carter, shepherd, cowherd, swineherd, gardener and harrower. Some of the women would be employed in domestic service. There would also be tradespeople such as blacksmiths and carpenters.

Although a relatively small place, Molescroft must have been a hamlet of much activity at this time. More people would be around and, one presumes that, with the establishment of friaries in Beverley, Dominican in 1240 and Franciscan in 1267, the Friars would make their appearances because it was their custom to move around the villages. This applied particularly to the Dominicans who were trained preachers. Their aim was to spread the Gospel amongst the ordinary people by the use of simple terms expressed in everyday language and, in consequence, they were well received. The priests viewed the Friars differently in that, by their taking on the role of teachers, they were usurping the responsibilities of the ordained ministry. Indeed, a statement deputed to have been issued by the Canons of the Collegiate Church describes the attitude of the time:

> 'You who listen to these friars are like geese listening to a fox and that will end for you in both temporal and spiritual ruin.'

It is superbly illustrated on one of the misericords in the Minster.

Amidst all that was happening there must have been great adversity, poverty, high infant mortality rate, diseases arising from malnutrition and poor housing, to name but a few causes. Presumably some of the men would be amongst those called upon to fight in the wars against the Scots – a long running feud arising from the attempted invasions of the English towns bordering on Scotland, a problem which persisted for many centuries and

MOLESCROFT AS IMAGINED

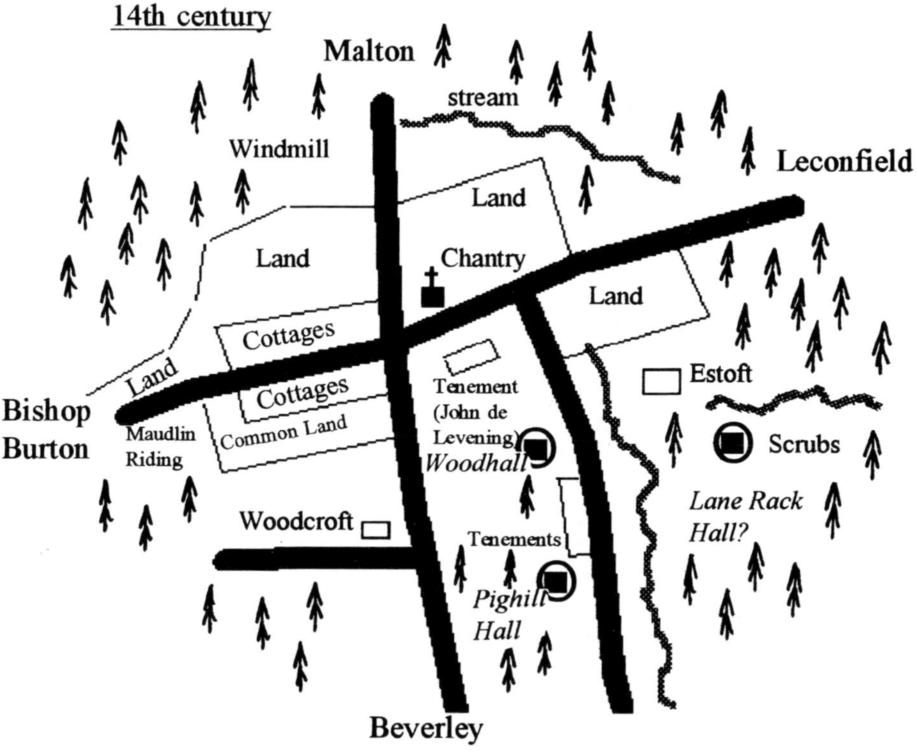

8th century
Malton
stream
Leconfield
stream
Bishop
Burton
cluster of
crude housing
Beverley

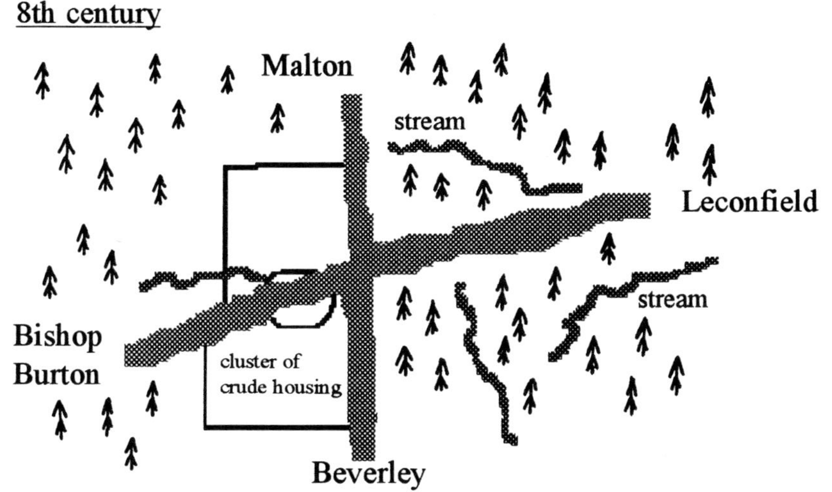

14th century
Malton
stream
Windmill
Leconfield
Land
Land
Chantry
Land
Cottages
Land
Cottages
Tenement
(John de
Levening)
Estoft
Bishop
Burton
Maudlin
Riding
Common Land
Woodhall
Scrubs
Lane Rack
Hall?
Woodcroft
Tenements
Pighill
Hall
Beverley

ending with the union of the two countries in 1603. *Bulmer's Directory*, (1892) states that in 1333 'Richard Dousing, Thomas de Holme and Adam Tyrwhit were appointed by the king to train all the able bodied men in Beverley in the use of arms and lead 50 horse and 50 foot soldiers against the Scots. Adam Copendale had to provide 100 soldiers.' Injuries and deaths would, no doubt, follow. Then there was the plague known as the Black Death which beset the whole country in 1348-1349 and the recurrences of 1361, 1369 and 1379, from which it is unlikely that the people of Molescroft escaped.

Despite these factors the adult population in 1377 was 99 according to the Poll Tax return of that date. Initially this seems a large number but, analysed more closely, it appears reasonable. There were at least six large houses with, say, six or eight adults in each, leaving, perhaps, 56 cottagers. Based on an average of four adults per cottage we arrive at a total of only 14 cottages.

The introduction of the Poll Tax in 1377 must have perturbed the peasants but when, in 1380, the annual payment was trebled from 1 groat to 3 groats and the contribution was the same for rich and poor alike, intense anger led to the Peasants' Revolt of 1381. It is said that there were only three isolated outbreaks in the North, one of which was in Beverley. Were the Molescroft peasants involved, I wonder? They would be well aware of the difference between their life style and that of their wealthier neighbours.

CHAPTER 3

15th and 16th CENTURIES

Unlike the two previous centuries, the 15th century provides no evidence of great changes in Molescroft, although one interesting feature is the entry of the Leedes family into its history. In the early part of the century Robert and William Leedes inherited Lane Rack Hall from Robert Ingleberd. Both were named amongst those for whom masses were to be said at the chantry. This, together with the inheritance, indicates that the Leedes family were closely related to the Ingleberds, Roger Ingleberd having founded the chantry in the previous century. In 1436 William Leedes died, and in his will, he stated that: 'He desires to be buried in the choir of the chapel of the blessed Mary at Beverley, near his wife.' (*Surtees Society Papers* 1855 Vol XXX). The grave slab is no longer evident. Robert Leedes held land of the Provost's fee which may have been granted as a reward for military service. This conjecture comes from the epitaph in the Minster's St. Katherine's Chapel on which he is described as 'Robert Leedes, Armigeri' – he was one who bore arms. The plaque is undated but research points to the likelihood of the two aspects being related. Molescroft has another relationship to St. Katherine's Chapel in that the house named Woodcroft formed part of the endowment of the preceding chantry established in 1450.

Houses and land continue to have a mention. In 1422 Estoft, previously owned by William Frost, passed to John Bedford, who also owned two tofts (homesteads) occupied by Thomas Wittie and John Hardy and 'lying between a common way which leads past the windmill' (probably on what is now Malton Road). St. Giles Hospital acquired land in Molescroft and the Knights Hospitallers are said to have owned a house, although I am not aware of the precise location. John Denton 'had a toft and croft', in other words, a house and smallholding.

A house without land was not a feasible proposition because of the need for self-sufficiency and hence the attraction of the rich fertile land of Molescroft. A supply of timber was another essential both for building purposes and for fuel so that wooded areas remained. Clearance would occur from time to time to meet an increased requirement for arable land. For example, a 10-acre wood at the Woodhall was cleared in the 15th century but a sizeable portion of woodland remained, at least, for the next 200 years.

One can picture a beautiful rural landscape but, at the same time, account has to be taken of the factors which marred the scene. Litter, garbage and waste would be cast out both from the large houses and from the cottages. Even the moats surrounding the large houses were used as receptacles for rubbish. Indeed, archaeologists find the unused moats of great interest, revealing such items as medieval pottery, wooden buckets and leather shoes.

The air would be pervaded constantly, not only by the odour emanating from the cast-out garbage but also by the smoke from the many domestic hearths, particularly when, in the 15th century, chimneys came into being, causing the smoke to spread more widely than when it emerged from windows and doorways, though this was likely to be wood smoke and less obnoxious than that from coal, which was not available at the time.

The 16th century heralded an era of great change brought about by the Reformation. Although a church reformation, it also represented social change, both of these aspects being demonstrated by such a small area as Molescroft because of its possession by the Church. The first impact of the Reformation was that the land held by St. Giles Hospital was relinquished as a result of the dissolution of the hospital, a religious house. This was followed in 1540 by the departure of the Knights Hospitallers because pilgrims were no longer going to the Minster; they had previously provided accommodation for them.

So we come to the date of the great change of 1548 resulting from the Chantries Act. It also applied to the Colleges, and consequently Beverley Minster ceased to be a Collegiate Church and became a Parish Church. Under the terms of the Act its wealth and its lands were annexed by the Crown and its estates became part of the Crown Manor of Beverley or were granted away. At this stage, the only exception was a very small area of five bovates handed to Beverley Corporation. The Chantry in Molescroft, like others, came to an end. Its last Chantry Priest was Robert Mote, who was retired with a pension of £4.11.8.

One significant result of the changed status of the Minster was that the Archbishop of York and the Provost were no longer the feudal lords. Similar situations occurred throughout the country so that replacement was necessary; hence the introduction in 1559 of Justices of the Peace, local gentry appointed by the Crown to govern the neighbourhood. A further important result of the changed situation was that the buying and selling of houses and land involved a different procedure. No longer did the transactions involve the 'making of suit at the Court of the Bedern' (that is at the Collegiate Church), but they were effected through the civil court. The would-be purchaser, known as the Plaintiff, had to initiate a suit at law against the existing owner (the Deforciant) by issuing a writ against him. In the *Yorkshire Archaeological and Topographical Association Record Series Volume III – Feet and Fines for the Tudor Period Part IV* it is recorded that, in 1549, Martin Rosse purchased a house with land at Moscrofte (*sic*) from Richard Jaklying and Elizabeth, his wife. The date, so soon after the Dissolution of the Collegiate Church, makes me reluctant to state categorically that the purchase followed the new procedure but the following two cases certainly did:

1594 John Wright, Gent, and Thomas Sherlock, Gent, purchased land from Robert Stockdale Esq.

1598 John Howe purchased a house and land from Henry Rosse, Gent.

A different aspect of land ownership is recorded in the *Victoria History of Beverley* where it is stated that, in 1585, the Crown granted three acres of land in Molescroft to St. Mary's Church – money from it to be used for the upkeep of the fabric.

In this century the legal requirement to maintain Church Registers of Baptisms, Marriages and Deaths was introduced. The Minster records date from 1559 so making it possible to glean some information about the people living in the area after careful scrutiny of the lengthy lists in order to extract details relative to Molescroft. The earliest entries in the Registers are somewhat brief but I used them, chiefly in an attempt to gain a rough idea of the size of the population. I estimate that around 36 families lived in the area in the 16th century. Interestingly, I traced some foreign sounding surnames such as Troffowil, Komissis, Connytio and Falios.

Apart from the Church Registers there is no available evidence relating to the peasantry. Based on the national situation it is assumed they would be living in cottages built of timber, with clay and rubble between the uprights, and cross beams. The earth floors would be covered with straw, a breeding ground for fleas and a danger to health as some fleas carried the plague. The sharing of their habitation with the animals continued, as the descriptive verse written about the housing at that time illustrates:

'Of one baye's breadth, God wot! a silly cote
Whose thatched sparres are furr'd with sluttish soote
A whole inch thick, shining like black-moor's brows
At his bed's head, feeding his stalled teme,
His swine beneath, his pullen ore the beame,
A starved tenement, such as I gesse
Stands stragling in the wasts of Holdernesse.'

(Written by Bishop Joseph Hall in the late 16th century and contained in the *Complete Poems* edited by A. B. Groshart, Manchester, 1879.)

CHAPTER 4

17th and 18th CENTURIES

The 17th century is sometimes regarded as the period marking the move toward the modern age but I find little to exemplify this in Molescroft. The important changes brought about by the Reformation had occurred in Molescroft in the previous century.

The buying and selling of land and houses continues to feature. In 1605 the land in Maudlin Riding which belonged formerly to Killingwoldgraves Hospital was bought by Sir William Gee. In the following year a part of the estate of the former chantry, including a mansion house and four cottages, was bought by Francis Morrice and Edmund Sawyer. The house named Woodcroft was sold in 1609 and, in 1669, the Manor of Woodhall, after going through several changes of ownership, was sold to Michael Warton by Thomas Beckwith. (The purchaser was the father of the more famous Sir Michael Warton who was a Member of Parliament for Beverley for many years and was a generous benefactor to the town and to the Minster.) Woodhall was a large estate but the largest was said to be that of the Taylor family.

One of the Taylor family, John, provides Molescroft with an interesting link with national affairs during the period of the Civil War, 1642-1649. In the *Yorkshire Archaeological Society Record Series*, Volume XV, 1893, it is stated that:

'John Taylor of Molescroft had to pay £54 before he could be released. Took the National Covenant in his Parish Church at Molescroft* and is certified by the Minister in his parish.

> Lands and Tenements lyinge and beinge in Molocroft (*sic*)
> His fine is £70.18.4.
> *(A mistake here, there being no Parish Church in Molescroft)'

The statement is an account of the action taken by the Parliamentarians against John Taylor because of his having fought on the side of the defeated Royalists. The petitioner had to obtain leave from the Committee for Compounding with Delinquents to compound, that is, to make a settlement of land and money to avoid prosecution. When granted, he had to submit his petition with the particulars of his estate and certificates verifying that he had taken the National Covenant and signed the Negative Oath.

In this context the Leedes family reappears with Robert Leedes being placed similarly to John Taylor as the following extract shows:

> 'ROBERT LEEDES OF MOLESCROFT ESQ.
> G198, p.229. Report – His delinquency that he left his habitation in the Kings quarters; he did render himself 26 Aug 1644. He

alledgeth he presented here his petition the last of Aug. which was referred 18 Feb. 1646; he took the Covenant 12 Aug. before Wm. Barton and the Oath here the same day. He is seized of lands in Molescroft and Beverley worth yearly £90.

1 March 1646 – R Gurdon   Rich. Shute
                                             Richard Vennar

Fine at a tenth £180   11 March 1646 (G4, p.38)

G198, p.232.   18 Feb 1646 PETITION Received

G198, p.233.   PARTICULARS OF ESTATE (As in the report)

G198, P.235.   27 Feb. 1646 CERTIFICATE from Fer. Fairfax.'

(Extracted from *Yorkshire Archaeological Society Record Series* Vol XVIII 1895, Royal Composition papers Vol II).

Robert Leedes died in 1656 and his wife, Elizabeth, died in 1680. It is recorded in Dugdale's *Visitation of Yorkshire* that both were 'buried at St. John's, Beverley', that is, in the Minster. I have been unable to trace their tomb slabs.

Their son, Engelbert, was baptised in the Minster on 24 April, 1633. He inherited the Lane Rack Hall estate in 1656 and, according to some sources, lived there until 1698. The latter date is in doubt because, again referring to Dugdale's *Visitation of Yorkshire*, it seems that, in 1666, Engelbert Leedes lived in North Milford Hall, near Tadcaster. This may be the date when the Leedes family ceased to occupy their Molescroft residence.

During the 17th century the Hearth Tax was repealed, a matter of interest as, at the time, there were 41 Hearth Tax payers in Molescroft and it would be right to regard this as an indication of the number of houses it contained. Judging from the Registers of Baptisms, Marriages and Burials it seems a reasonable assumption, as I found the names of 36 families entered for the period 1607-1622.

From June, 1610, to November, 1611, there was a severe outbreak of plague in Beverley. Its severity can be judged by the entry in the Registers of St. Mary's Church stating that '32 people were buried of the plague besides 40 that was shuffled into graves without any reading over them at all'. I cannot report to what extent the people of Molescroft were affected by the terrible epidemic but I doubt they would escape it.

The Church Registers of the 18th century provide more helpful details than previously, with the inclusion of the employment against each entry. This enabled the drawing-up of the following list:

Ale House Keeper	1	Labourers	20
Blacksmith	1	Miller	1
Carpenter	2	Poulterer	1
Cartwright	1	Servant	1
Farmer	8	Tailor	1
Gardener	1	Thatcher	4
Glover	1	Weaver	2

A few of the descriptions against the entries are rather strange, for example:

BAPTISM	1778	Sarah Bacchus and Phoebe, her daughter, two black women
DEATHS	1718	John Gooseman, a stranger from Molescroft
	1718	Wm Dudding, a poor man of Molescroft
	1725	A stranger unknown from Molescroft

The name of the Ale House Keeper, Stephen Kirkham, first appears in 1715 when his son's baptism is recorded, but it is not until 1754 that the first mention of the public house appears, known at that date as the Marquis of Wellington.

And so we return to the houses and land transactions. In 1719, according to a Deed held in the County Record Office there was the following Assignment of Lease:

> 'Romington Farms late in the occupation of Wm. Bell. Rented by John and Thomas Anther for a term of 8 years from Wm Taylor at a rent of £39 per year – sub-let to Ellerington, house and grazing £21 per year.'

The main estates, those of the Taylors, Lord Langdale and the Wartons, each have a place in 18th-century history. In 1731 the Taylor estate passed to Mr. Taylor's daughter, Bridget, the wife of Ralph Pennyman. By 1750 it is reported as comprising nine houses, 100+ acres of land, and many separate closes. After Mrs. Pennyman's death it passed to her surviving sisters but towards the end of the century much of the estate was bought by Sir Christopher Sykes of Sledmere.

The size of the Langdale estate in 1770 was 179 acres. It was owned by Lord Langdale until his death in 1778 when it passed to his wife, Constantia, and, on her death in 1792, to her daughters, Lady Stourton of Wiltshire, the Hon. Elizabeth Butler of London and Lady Clifford of Chudleigh.

The Warton estate provides two pieces of information. In 1775 ownership passed to Michael Newton, nephew of the former owner, Susannah Warton. An aid to picturing the estate is the information that in the late 18th century it had 600 trees, mainly oak. In 1736 James Grayburn of Elm Tree Farm (Church Road) bought 70 acres of land. Unfortunately I do not know from whom he bought it. The farm house was built in the 18th century and re-modelled in the 19th century.

Another house of historic interest is Swiss Cottage (No. 49 Molescroft Road) which, according to its present owner, existed in 1762 in the form of two cottages which had been joined into one, plus a barn and land. At that time it was occupied by John and Mary Wright, six years later by Matthew

Rimington, followed in 1772 by Henry Bell and, in 1794, by Elizabeth, the wife of Thomas Bugg. It is likely that it was one of several houses in that particular area as described in the following chapter where further reference to Swiss Cottage is made.

One source indicates that the 18th century saw the demise of one of the largest houses, namely Pighill Hall, in 1759 but, according to a Deed held in the County Record Office, that appears to be incorrect. In 1797 it is recorded that the Manor of Pighill was sold to Robert Rigby. The wording of the Deed describes it as

> 'Of all that's the scitre of the Capital Messuage, mansion or manor houses called Pighill Hall, moated round and all that close called Dove Cote close adjoining thereto plus Ash Garth together with the Pithos received.'

In 1799 the two closes were 'transferred' to William Beverley and John Lockwood.

A previous occupant of Pighill Hall was Thomas Clarke who, in the latter half of the century, had Molescroft House (formerly Cottage), built on the site of a cottage which he purchased in 1766 from Christopher Thornton, a tailor. The tomb slab of the Clarke family can be seen in the North Transept of the Minster.

Molescroft Road, still very rural at the turn of the century, with Elmsall Lodge in the background

MOLESCROFT LAND PRIOR TO ENCLOSURE, 1803

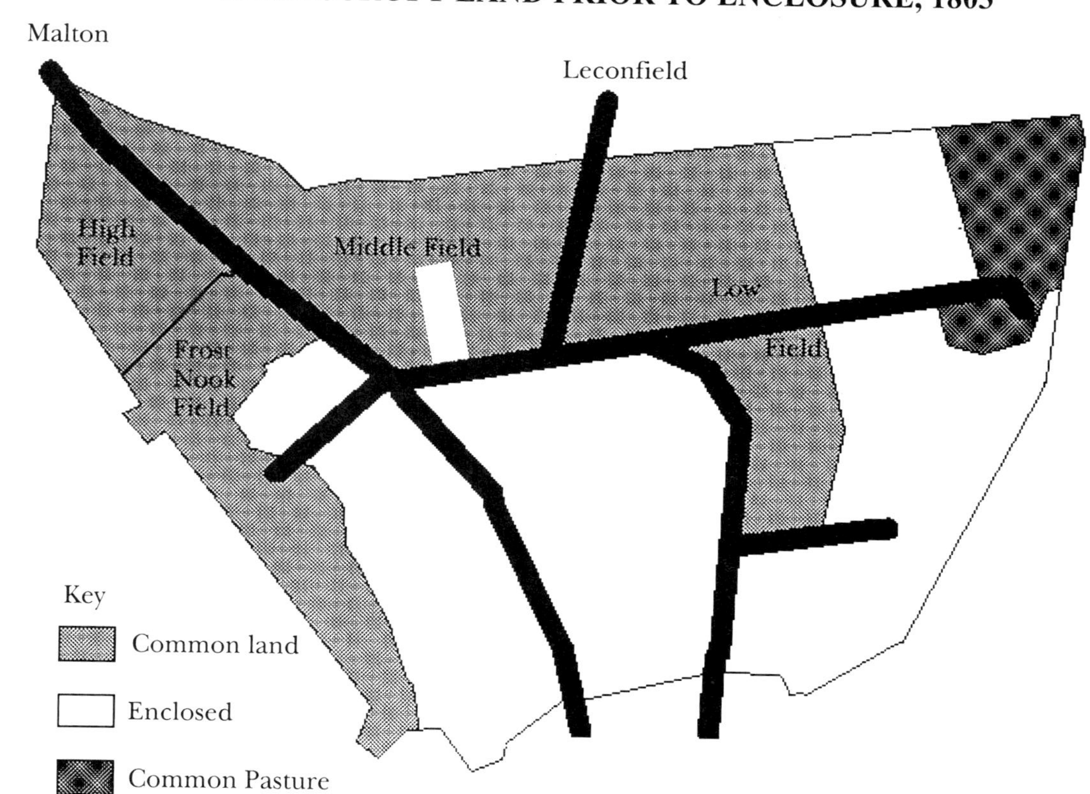

CHAPTER 5

19th CENTURY

1801 was the year of the first ten-yearly Census of Population, making it possible to state with far greater certainty that the number of inhabitants of Molescroft was then 67. Many of these would be cottagers who relied on their access to the common lands for much of their food as their strips of land in the large fields were essential to their cultivation of vegetables and grain. The commons also provided grazing ground for cattle and other animals. Such fields in Molescroft numbered four: High Field and Frost Nook field to the north-west, Middle Field in the north and Low Field on the north-eastern side. (As late as 1854 the now Woodhall Way was named Low Field Road because it ran along the edge of that field.) At this time the total area of Molescroft was 1,360 acres, of which approximately 50% was common land. It is interesting to note the extension to the acreage since the entry in the Domesday Book, which showed it to be slightly more than 300.

The farming of the four named fields was to change when, in 1803, under the Enclosure Act of that date, the common lands were granted to the existing landowners. The following details give a rough idea of the apportionment:

	Acres
Sir Mark Sykes	319
The Langdale Estate	238
Wm Grayburn (Elm Tree Farm)	89
St. Mary's Church	4 (includes the 3 acres granted by the Crown in 1585)
Others	36
	686

From the cottagers' viewpoint this was a sad situation as it marked the end of their self-sufficiency, and they were powerless to seek adequate compensation for the loss of their strips in the open fields and the pasture for their animals. The financial problem was increased by its occurring at a time when labourers' wages were low. An indication of poverty in Molescroft is that, in 1800, there was a cottage used as a Poor House. (The area was independent of the Beverley Poor Law Union until 1836.)

On the other hand, enclosure was beneficial to farming in that the dispersed and fragmented holdings of the common land were replaced by individually managed fields which were easier to work and provided flexibility in the use of the land. The former open fields were divided by hedges to form rectangular fields facilitating the rotation of crops and providing improved pasture. In effect it was the birth of farming as we know it today.

The pattern of farms was gradually established and, in the first half of the 19th century, there developed:

Elm Tree Farm
Molescroft Grange (Carr Close Farm, Lowfield Farm)
Constitution Hill Farm
Molescroft Carr Farm
Manor Farm

Enclosure and the clearance of much of the woodland changed the face of Molescroft but other features appearing during the century contributed to the beginning of its development. One of these is housing because of the attraction of living on the higher ground on Molescroft Road. 1812 saw the appearance of Molescroft Cottage, occupied by the Wainewright family, followed by a property described as 'a dwellinghouse with a stable, outbuildings, yard and garden,' (now identified as 71/73 Molescroft Road) which was built in 1816 by a wealthy owner of property and land, Edward Ashley, who had bought a large part of the holding of Sir Mark Sykes.

A useful aid to imagining the Molescroft of this era is provided by a report in the *Hull Advertiser,* 27 July, 1821, relating to the celebrations of the coronation of George IV:

> 'At Molescroft village near Beverley, the Union Jack was displayed by Lt. Renon R.N. from his cottage. Upon the grass oppôsite the labourers and their wives were regaled with beef and ale, the children partook of plum cake and tea, and the day was celebrated by innocent amusements.
>
> '*God Save the King*' with a dance, ushered in the evening.'

A return to 71/73 Molescroft Road. Its particular interest is attributable to George Doyle who occupied part of it from 1851 to 1894 and herein lies the origin of the one house becoming two. George's sister, Georgina Tindall, had moved into 71/73 Molescroft Road in 1850 as a tenant and, when George went to live with her, it was decided that he should have his own separate accommodation in what was, probably, the part built as a stable. George was an ardent devotee of the Gothic style of architecture resulting from his great admiration for Beverley Minster. In consequence he went so far as to build a Gothic facade on his part of the property. In addition, he put in a stained glass window showing the date of the innovation and installed a public clock with a bell which could be heard by the inhabitants of the area. George will be mentioned again when the subject of the church in Molescroft is dealt with.

It seems from the list of properties bought by Edward Ashley in 1814 that there were four cottages on the north side of the public house so that the north-west end of Molescroft Road, continuing into Church Street, was fully built up by the latter half of the century. The public house, no doubt, has an interesting history as it seems that, until the latter part of the century, it was an inn, judging from the title given to the person who was in charge. For example, in 1836 Mr. P. Downes was known as the innkeeper, signifying that accommodation was provided. Perhaps J. and S. Boswell, described as travellers, stayed there . In 1851 Hannah Battle had the title of victualler, indicating that she was a provider of food. Finally, in 1891, James Hewitt is recorded as a publican. During this period the public house, originally known as the Marquis of Wellington, underwent two changes of name. By 1840, when Francis Johnson was in charge, it was the Trafalgar and in 1875 became the Molescroft. As a central feature in the area it is appropriate so to have named it.

Despite the additional housing, the number of dwellings recorded at the time of the 1851 Census of Population was still only 31. Some were situated in an area bounded by Church Road and Robinson's Lane. The lane no longer exists but, judging from a map of 1840, it ran from about mid-way along Church Road (known as Towngate or Town Street), circling the back of Swiss Cottage, and joining Molescroft Road in the Gallows Lane area. Indentures of 1853 in the County Archives detail four cottages and three houses set around the area which presents a picture not unlike that of some modern arrangements

Molecroft Inn , earlier this century.

of residences. I have not traced the precise date of origin of all the housing but it is likely that some were built in the previous century along with Swiss Cottage.

The occupants of the houses at the time of the indenture were Thomas Brigham, William Locke and John Scrivener, who each lived in one of the three 'tenements or dwellinghouses with the yards, gardens and premises and the orchard and piece of ground attached thereto'. They were part of the estate of William and John Bugg which they had inherited from their father, Thomas Bugg. Another part of his estate was Swiss Cottage which, in the year 1800, was occupied by him and later by his sons. Of the other cottages the occupancy of only two is clear when Francis Smith and William Gray are quoted as holding the tenure. The owner was probably John Christopher Cankrien, who also owned land in the area. In 1853 he and other members of the family purchased all the properties detailed and took up residence in Swiss Cottage, presumably suitably adapted to their needs.

By 1851 the population was 133, double that of 50 years earlier: the main contributory factor appears to be movement into Molescroft. 84% of the residents came from outside the area, a few from relatively long distances away, such as Newcastle and Thetford, Norfolk, others from the surrounding villages and from Hull. An analysis of the details of the types of employment quoted in the Census helps towards an appreciation of the early beginnings of a changing Molescroft. The movement towards a residential area is demonstrated by the fact that amongst the inhabitants are a surgeon dentist (William Henry Dulton), a solicitor (Joseph Walker), and an auctioneer (Francis Stamp). Three people were entered as annuitants, one of them, Rosamund Dixon, being described also as a landowner.

The more efficient use of the land may provide the reason for the large increase in the number of agricultural labourers since the previous century. In 1851 there were 34, a few being children of 11 years and upwards. Of the other children, eight ranging in age from five to 13 years, are listed as scholars. Female employment is mainly restricted to domestic service – the number in this group being seven.

Additionally there are farmers, a blacksmith, dressmaker, groom, nurseryman and the victualler, in the earlier century identified as the ale house keeper. Other categories indicate changing times: a bricklayer (but no thatcher) and the toll gate keeper, Joseph Waite, who originated from Bradford.

The first toll gate, or turnpike, keeper is mentioned in the Church Registers as Mr. T. Harrison, whose son was baptised in 1831. The turnpike road, established in 1830, began at the boundary with St. Mary's Parish, that is, at the Gallows Lane junction with Molescroft Road, and extended 288 yards into the Driffield Road and 165 yards into the Malton Road. This was the only surfaced road in Molescroft and, in consequence, would be much used by horse-drawn vehicles of varying kinds, so involving costly maintenance. Prior to the turnpike being installed the cost of maintenance of the road had to be met by the Civil Parish, an absurd situation when the greatest users would be travellers from a distance, often with vehicles bearing heavy loads. Consequently the Parish was reluctant or unable to bear the cost of maintenance. Hence turnpike companies were granted parliamentary powers to erect gates and toll bars to enable the collection of charges from road users.

This system highlights the inadequacy of the existing means of local government in the absence of a specific method of rating. Rural areas were still governed by Justices of the Peace who were responsible for deciding upon the raising and use of local rates. Their responsibilities ranged widely yet they had no effective bureaucracy to carry out local administration. It was not until 1888 when, under the Local Government Act of that date, a more democratically elected County Council came into being, followed in 1894 by Rural District Councils, Molescroft becoming part of Beverley Rural District.

One financial burden, that is, the cost of road maintenance, was probably reduced by the coming of the railway to the area, providing an alternative means of transporting heavy loads. In 1846 the line to Bridlington was opened, followed, in 1865, by the one to Market Weighton. Not everyone would view such an innovation with pleasure as people witnessed the intrusion on the land and were concerned about the effect on their way of life. George Eliot's *Middlemarch* (first published 1871/72) includes a graphic account of the reaction of some villagers and I quote just one of the many statements made about the railway:

> 'And all for the big traffic to swallow up the little, so there shan't be a team left on the land, nor a whip to crack.'

I wonder if similar sentiments were being expressed in Molescroft. If so, then they are in sharp contrast with to-day's appreciation of the practical value of the railway leading to consideration being given to Molescroft having its own railway station or, at least, a Halt.

Did the poorer people of Molescroft gain anything from the modernisation taking place around them? Their cottages were, perhaps, a little more comfortable and the Public Health Act of 1848 would, ultimately, result in the reduction of disease and fewer early deaths. The lack of any opportunity for education was one of the serious detriments but an attempt to alleviate it was made in 1831 when an infants school was opened. It is likely that it would be established in a house and be a dame school where reading, writing and arithmetic were taught for a small fee. It is recorded that the usual attendance was six boys and eight girls, which would represent only a proportion of the population of children. Not every family would be able to afford the fee nor would some feel the need to do so. The school existed for some 40 years, its closure probably being a result of the Education Act 1870 which effectively began the system of compulsory education. No longer having a school in Molescroft, the children had to travel to the town, on foot presumably, to attend the Minster National Schools. Such apparent inconvenience should not, however, detract from the tremendous advantage brought about by compulsory education. A clear illustration is shown in the 1891 Census of Population where 38 children are now described as 'Scholars'. This important change is but one of many in the rapid development of Molescroft. In the 40 years from 1851, the population increased by 56% to 196, which meant additional housing and the total number of houses reaching 42.

Amongst those built in the period was Longcroft Hall at the top of Gallows Lane. Its first occupant was Mr. J. A. Hudson, the son of a brickmaker from Hull. It is no longer a residence but forms part of the complex of the Beverley College. In 1879 Elmsall Lodge (No. 30 Molescroft Road) was built for Henry Dixon, a silk merchant from Hull, and later purchased by Harry Wray, a well-known civic figure in Beverley. The house is now a residential home for the elderly, known as Molescroft Court. At about this time there appeared additional housing in Church Road when five cottages known as Thompson's Place were built. According to a newspaper cutting reporting the sale of the houses in 1917, the total annual rent was £34.14.0 making the weekly rent for each house to be 2s.8d. (14p).

Other changes are shown in the 1891 Census. In looking at the various means of livelihood one is attracted by the increase in the types of employment. In 1851 there were 16, but 40 years later they numbered 27. There were now only nine agricultural labourers, not that the farms would be reduced significantly in acreage but, presumably, there would be the beginnings of mechanisation. Moving on to a different sphere one finds that, by 1891, more professional people were living in the area, among them a professor and teacher of wood carving (William James T. Horley), an English

Toll Bar Cottage, built 1830 at the junction of Gallows Lane and Molescroft Road.

tutor (William Edward Hare), and an artist and portrait painter, John Harold Hudson, the son of Mr. J. A. Hudson J.P. who lived in Longcroft Hall. There was still a resident from the legal profession but now it was a barrister, Mill Stevenson. There were seven people described as 'living on own means'. Two members of the Police Force lived in Molescroft, Richard Taylor, described as a Police Officer, and a Police Constable named Robert Sharp. Jockeys numbered two, one of whom, Frederick Charles Horley, was the son of the teacher of wood carving. The platelayer, William Richardson, probably worked on the section of the railway close to Molescroft. A church sexton also resided in the area. To complete the list of occupations not previously mentioned, there were the joiner, plus his apprentice, and a butler. The women must not be omitted as those who had paid employment were assets to the community – three dressmakers, four laundresses and eight in domestic service: a small representation of the total number of females but the remainder would be fully occupied in the home.

Amidst all the changes taking place, in particular the increasing population, there was, as yet, no local Anglican church and the need was not met until nearing the close of the century. Meanwhile attendance at the 'far off' Parish Church, the Minster, presented a difficulty for those without means of transport.

A picturesque description of the existing situation is provided by George Oliver in 1829:

> 'The parishes of Beverley, in addition to the great distance which many of the inhabitants of St. John's reside from the church, are interwoven in a most intricate and curious manner. Their intersections do not tend so much to the convenience as the benefit of the parishioners, if extended exercise be considered an advantage. The inhabitants of Molescroft pass the open doors of the church of St. Mary on their way to their own parish church, the minster; and many of the parishioners of St. Nicholas, whose legitimate place of worship is St. Mary's, in like manner, pass the minster on their way thither. In the summer season this is attended with no inconvenience, but is rather replete with gratification. It is pleasant on the Sabbath day to see the streets crowded with human beings, devoutly proceeding to the house of prayer to celebrate their deliverance from moral slavery and eternal death; it is pleasant for friend to salute friend as they cross each other's path when passing to their respective churches; but in winter, when the rain falls, or the bleak wind rushes with thrilling coldness through the streets, some friendly arrangements might give the inhabitants of each parish access to the nearest church that no individual may be deprived of the delightful employment of joining in the public exercise of religion, by considerations of distance or extremity of weather, in that inclement season.'

ELMSALL
LODGE

Molescroft, however, was not deprived entirely of its places of worship. As early as the 1820s the Wesleyan Methodists held services there and it is recorded that, at a later date, a preaching station was established by the Particular Baptists. George Doyle, mentioned earlier in relation to his house in Molescroft Road, took the initiative and, between 1848 and 1851, used the kitchen of his sister's home, a farm house in Church Road, for the holding of services. It is said that 'a local clergyman' conducted the services and choirboys from the Minster provided the music. The latest date in this list is 1883 when services were held in a hired Mission Room although I do not know its whereabouts.

Perhaps all this was partly responsible for the decision to provide an Anglican church. Molescroft was of inadequate size for a new Ecclesiastical Parish to be created but the problem was solved in 1896 by the building of a chapel of ease to the Minster. The church, dedicated to St. Leonard, was built at the junction of the Malton and Driffield roads being, at that time, in close proximity to the majority of the housing. It is significant that the site is probably that of the former chantry.

The century closed with there being some 200 inhabitants, showing a threefold increase since the beginning of the century. The land belonged to:

William Bainton, Beverley Parks
E. R. B. Hall-Watt, Bishop Burton
Henry Horn Almack, Long Milford, Suffolk
Thomas C. Dixon, Brandesburton
J. A. Hudson, Molescroft.

St. Leonard's Church, Molescroft, early 20th century.

CHAPTER 6

20th CENTURY

The final section of this historical account could be entitled 'the age of great development', illustrated by the twentyfold rise in population in this 20th century when agricultural land was sold and occupied, in the main, by houses.

The 'great development' began in the 1930s but there was one large house built prior to that, Molescroft Hall at the north-eastern end of Molescroft Road, erected in 1900 for Mr. Richard Hodgson. (It has been demolished recently and the ground is being built upon.) Apart from that, there was no significant amount of building taking place in the first three decades of the century, although there was a population increase of 58. In the early 1930s a part of the Pighill estate was sold for housing along Pighill Lane and the rest of the land exchanged hands several times before it succumbed to housing. Building in Westfield Avenue also began in the 1930s. I am intrigued by the importance of this period and the reasons for its marking the origin of the modern Molescroft. The factors which come to mind are the attraction of a modern house at an affordable price, the rural location, the comparatively low domestic rate applicable in the Rural District and the increase in car ownership which would offset the inconvenience of living at a distance from the town. It was, presumably, the growth of housing which prompted the establishment of the Parish Council in 1937. The following year saw the building of council houses in Church Road.

The Second World War prevented further development. There was just one minor event in 1940, the renaming of Pighill Lane as Woodhall Way. One can imagine that Molescroft would not be without excitement, not least because the people would be very aware of the presence of 616 Squadron RAF stationed at Leconfield. The flight path, necessary at that time, was over Molescroft and land was left open for this purpose. It was not until 1977 that the last of such land was sold by the Ministry of Defence. Building was resumed in 1948, with houses on the west side including Longcroft Park and also housing in Woodhall Way, Driffield Road and Church Street. Housing continued in the 1950s; indeed, the rate of provision accelerated. By 1951 the population had increased by 164% over the previous 20 years to reach 689 but, in the following ten years, it more than doubled to 1,453.

Amongst the events of the decade was the official opening of Longcroft County Secondary School in 1950 to accommodate pupils from the town and the surrounding villages. This was followed in 1958 by Molescroft County Secondary School built nearby to serve as Longcroft Lower School. Two years later the two were combined under one title, Longcroft School. There was, as yet, no primary school in Molescroft, so that children had to wait until they were 11 years of age before enjoying the benefit of a school in their own area. Another feature was the establishment, in 1952, of a sewage plant in Ings

Road, Molescroft, presumably a result of the massive increase in population.

In the following decade, the first significant date is that of 1960 when the Beverley Technical Institute (now the Beverley College) was established in Gallows Lane. The growth in the number of houses continued until, by 1969, the majority of the ground between Molescroft Road and Woodhall Way had been built over. In 1969 the 45 council houses in Hillcrest and Woodhall Way were built.

Such continuing growth in population, which was to reach 2,738 by 1971, warranted the provision of shopping facilities. So a parade of six shops was built in 1965, catering for most everyday needs – a fish and chip shop, supermarket, hairdresser, newsagent with sub post office, wine and spirit and a laundrette. Another event in 1965 was the closure of the railway line from Beverley to Market Weighton, indicating the expansion of road transport which caused the line to be far less essential.

More houses were still appearing in the 1970s although at a lesser rate than previously. For example, some were located at the higher end of Woodhall Way, in The Croft and the extended Hillcrest Drive. One of the former 'flight path' sites was built upon, involving additional houses in Woodhall Way and Hillcrest Drive. The population increase in this decade decelerated to only 15%. There were, however, other additions taking place. The Playing Field in Woodhall Way was opened in 1971. 1975 is an important date for it was in that year that, after a lapse of a century, Molescroft, once again, had a school. It is a County Primary School to accommodate 200 pupils of 5-11 years of age. The provision of a Parish Centre within the school forms a most welcome asset for the community.

In the year prior to that the Beverley Rural District Council came to an end and the rating of Molescroft came under Beverley Borough. The effect was financial as the benefit of the former low rural rate was lost. Coincidental with the changeover, the era of the separate sewage plant ended and the system reverted to the town's system. The local plant would, in any event, it is presumed, have been inadequate to cope with the existing circumstances, having in mind that there had been a fourfold increase in population during the 20 years it had been in existence.

The continuing increase in population meant that the church of St. Leonard's was proving too small. This was evident, particularly, at such times as Easter and Harvest Festival when extra chairs and other forms of seating were brought in to fill every available space in an attempt to accommodate the congregation. Consequently, in 1979, the church was extended to a maximum seating capacity of 72. At the same time some modernisation took place with new chairs, new carpet and a modern organ. An apt addition to the east wall is a large wooden cross kindly presented by the Army School of Mechanical Transport, Leconfield. The church also contains two memorials. A tablet on the north wall commemorates Miss Christiana Stead 'Who in the service of God worked for this Parish for over 35 years'. I understand that she was a

Sunday School teacher in the earlier part of this century. The other memorial, of more recent date, is in the form of a font cover and commemorates Miss Doris Gliddon who was in charge of the Sunday School for many years, in addition to being the church organist. The seating capacity of 72 should not be taken as representing the total number of persons in Molescroft who attend Church. The Parish Church is the Minster, and hence some worship there and others spread amongst the many other churches in the town and, perhaps, beyond in a few cases.

At this stage the modern Molescroft seems complete but there was still a large area of ground to the east of Woodhall Way as yet unused. In the 1980s this was transformed into an attractive housing complex forming a major extension and a consequent further rise in population to around 4,000 by the close of the decade. One advantage of the new development is that it gives a convenient pedestrian access to Norwood. In this period also, a local bus service was initiated, a most useful link with the town.

On 15 December, 1994, a new major road was opened by Councillor Veronica Wilson, Chair of Humberside County Council. Constructed on the northern side, it links Swinemoor Lane and Hull Bridge Road with Driffield Road and is a means of easing the traffic flow through the town. In association with this significant addition to Molescroft another 1,000 or so houses are to be built in the vicinity of the new road, and another population rise is due. The resultant changes belong to the future.

Molescroft Hall, erected 1900 for Mr. Richard Hodgson, now demolished.